C000185976

PERSONAL DEVELOPMENT
WITH THE
I ☯ CHING
A NEW INTERPRETATION

PERSONAL DEVELOPMENT
WITH THE
I CHING
A NEW INTERPRETATION

PAUL SNEDDON

quantum
LONDON • NEW YORK • TORONTO • SYDNEY

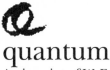

quantum

An imprint of W. Foulsham & Co. Ltd
The Publishing House, Bennetts Close,
Cippenham, Slough, Berkshire, SL1 5AP, England

Dedicated to the memory of my much-respected father, James Sneddon, whose wisdom and advice have sustained me in all my endeavours, and to my mother Isabel, from whom I inherited compassion for my fellow human beings. My thanks go also to my soul-mate Penny, with whom I have finally found fulfilment.

ISBN 0–572–02796-6

Copyright © 1990 and 2003 Paul Sneddon

Cover illustration by Jurgen Ziewe

Previously published as *Self-development with the I Ching*

All rights reserved.

The moral right of the author has been asserted.

The Copyright Act prohibits (subject to certain very
limited exceptions) the making of copies of any copyright work
or of a substantial part of such a work, including the making of
copies by photocopying or similar process. Written permission
to make a copy or copies must therefore normally be obtained from
the publisher in advance. It is advisable also to consult the
publisher if in any doubt as to the legality of any copying
which is to be undertaken.

Printed in Great Britain by St Edmundsbury Press, Bury St Edmunds, Suffolk

Contents

Introduction

The *I Ching* is the ancient Chinese book of wisdom and divination, known as the *Book of Changes*. For thousands of years it has been used by the Chinese as an oracle – something to consult as a source of wisdom to help your decision-making and expand your knowledge of the future. As such, although it would appear initially to fit into the category of fortune-telling, along with tarot cards, palmistry and astrology, it is far older than any of these. In addition, its readings are often uncannily accurate, and this explains why it has been called the ultimate oracle.

It has been said that the *I Ching* owes its success to the fact that its pronouncements are almost entirely composed of platitudes, mostly vague, and that it is easy to read any interpretation into their amorphous content. At first sight, this may appear to be the case. The situation is further complicated by the flowery language and obscure terminology of the original text, although it must be remembered that the *I Ching* was written thousands of years ago, in the language of the day. In the same way, the pronouncements were formed within the context of events at that time. Many of the original pronouncements, therefore, relate to the antiquated symbolism of battles, feudal princes and foreign animals. Phrases indicating good or bad omens and success or failure were used to assist the practice of divination.

In the thousands of years since the book was written, many eminent scholars have translated it from Chinese into Latin, German, English, and a host of other languages. In recent years several attempts have been made to render it into modern-day language, but none has succeeded in retaining the depth of meaning that the *I Ching* contains. The reader has therefore been faced either with having to flounder in a sea of obscure language, in the case of earlier versions, or with having to accept the more incomplete meanings of later versions.

In the last few decades, interest in the *I Ching* has spread to the West, and the book has many followers who treat its judgements with considerable seriousness. It seemed to me regrettable that the nature of the book's text was excluding a much greater following. I therefore set myself the task of simplifying the book, by translating it into language and terminology accessible to and appropriate for the modern reader.

Assisted by the copious notes of previous scholars, I carefully removed all the old symbolism and reference to battles, princes and foreign animals, without detracting in any way from the context of the original. In doing so, I took great care not to fall into the trap of translating the book into modern-day language only to make its relevance solely applicable to the present day.

This version of the *I Ching*, which I refer to as the *New I Ching*, removes entirely the vagueness of the original readings whilst retaining in its entirety the meaning of the text. The answers obtained by using the *New I Ching* will be much more to the point and it is hoped that this new version will encourage the use of the book by many more people.

I Ching and the Concept of Change

The *I Ching* or *Book of Changes* is aptly named: it is a book that charts the changes that occur continuously in life. To understand what the ancient authors meant by change, you need some insight into Eastern thought. The human brain is split into two hemispheres, left and right, separated by a large nerve track called the *corpus callosum*. Whereas we in the West mostly use the left hemisphere, the 'reality-testing' side, people born in the Eastern world make more use of the right hemisphere, the 'imagination' side. We are all born with the same kind of brain. It is our upbringing that determines the side that we favour. In the West, children initially use the 'imagination' side of the brain, but we are taught as we grown older to suppress the imagination in favour of more rational, logical thought. In the East this does not happen to the same extent.

This is best illustrated in the differing approaches of East and West to problems. Whereas in the West we tend to approach them in a straightforward, logical manner, the Eastern approach is more imaginative, and indirect.

In a contest, the Westerner will attempt to win by considering how best victory may be achieved in the shortest possible time. In contrast, the Easterner will try to anticipate the actions of the opponent, in order both to obstruct such actions and also to turn them to personal advantage. The recent growth in popularity in the West of martial arts provides us with an example. In a fight, the Westerner will consider only how to bring an opponent to the ground in the quickest fashion. The Easterner will wait for and anticipate the blow and will attempt to use the opponent's own actions against them, by moving with, rather than against, the impetus of the blow.

The belief that it is more sensible to move *with* the forces of nature rather than against them, is a sound attitude. For thousands of years, the Chinese have symbolised the opposing forces of nature as Yin and Yang. Even today, many ailments are attributed to either an excess or deficit of Yin or Yang in the body.

Yin symbolises shade, Yang, light. Yin is used to describe the female or passive elements, Yang, the male, or active. In Western terms, Yin is negative, Yang, positive. Many Chinese believe that life and nature consist of a flow between Yin and Yang and that everything is constantly changing. As the seasons occur and reoccur, so does life consist successively of cycles of destruction and reconstruction.

The *I Ching* teaches how the 'Chuntzu' or 'Superior Person' should behave. It states that the proper and good life is achieved when life is in harmony with the flux of Yin and Yang and when moves are made in agreement with the continuous advance and retreat of the vital forces of nature. In this way, an expanding awareness and universal spirit can be achieved.

To be in harmony with the flow of nature, one must also be reconciled to the concept of cyclic change. In the West, we fight change whenever and wherever it occurs, believing basically that change is bad. Even change that is obviously for the better, we view with suspicion and dislike.

Change, however, is inevitable. Cyclic change is even more so. Nature is built upon cyclic change: as winter follows summer, as night follows day, so occur the changes in every aspect of life. Things cannot continually improve nor continually decay. There has to be an end somewhere, a breathing space. At that point, reversal sets in and the process begins anew. So it is with life itself. Birth is, without exception, followed by death. Good is followed by bad; bad by good. History shows that peace is always followed by war; war by peace. Fashions die out, only to reappear later.

Only by accepting the inevitability of, and by conforming to, cyclic change, can harmony be achieved and peace of mind attained. This is the basic principle behind the concept of change in the *I Ching*.

The History of the I Ching

The *I Ching* is a collection of 64 short essays based on ancient Chinese philosophy. A question is asked and the throwing of sticks or coins results in the random selection of one of the essays, which is then supposed to relate in some way to the question. The essays are represented by 64 symbolic figures known as 'hexagrams'. These are composed of two 'trigrams', each of which comprises three broken or solid lines. It is interesting that some two thousand years elapsed between the devising of the trigrams and the devising of the hexagrams.

In 3322 BC, the Emperor Fu-hsi chose to indicate the difference between the two opposing forces of nature by using a broken line (━━ ━━) to represent Yin, and a solid line (━━━━━) to represent Yang. For whatever reason, he then created four new figures by combining broken and solid lines (━━ ━━ , ━━ ━━ , ━━━━━ , ━━━ ━━). His next step was to create the trigrams, by adding either a broken or solid line to each of these four figures. In this way the eight trigrams were formed. Fu-hsi also gave a name, image, attribute and symbol to each trigram (see page 11).

It is easy to see how the ancient authors linked the attributes to the images and symbols. A mountain is obviously an obstacle, something that prevents progress. The flames of a fire are bright and beautiful. In thunder there is an element of movement and of danger.

These trigrams have been called the most ancient expressions of the human mind. Possibly they are – they were certainly in use five thousand years ago. Tortoiseshells have been unearthed, dating back to that period, on which are inscribed the eight trigrams. There is also some evidence to suggest that the trigrams were used as an early aid to divination.

THE EIGHT TRIGRAMS

Trigram	Name	Attribute	Image	Symbol
	Ch'ien	creative, male, active	heaven	father
	K'un	receptive, female, passive	earth	mother
	Chen	movement, danger	thunder	1st son
	K'an	pit, danger	water	2nd son
	Ken	prevention of progress	mountain	3rd son
	Sun	gentle force	wood, wind	1st daughter
	Li	brightness, beauty	fire	2nd daughter
	Tui	satisfaction	marsh, lake	3rd daughter

Over the next two thousand years, the Chinese developed their remarkable early culture. In 2850 BC the legendary Golden Age of China began. The Hsia dynasty commenced in 2205 BC, to be followed by the Shang dynasty in 1600 BC, and subsequently the Chou dynasty in 1027 BC. It was in the closing years of the Shang dynasty that the hexagrams were first formed, by the founder of the Chou dynasty, King Wen.

In the year 1143 BC King Wen was imprisoned by the emperor in Yu-li, in the province of Ho-nan. In this and the following year he worked on combining the trigrams to form hexagrams. Using all eight trigrams, in every permutation, he came up with the 64 hexagrams, as illustrated on pages 13–15.

Several of the hexagrams appear to have the same Chinese names. This is due to the subtle peculiarities of the Chinese language; the English equivalents show that the actual meanings are completely different. King Wen went on to interpret the meanings of the hexagrams and composed 64 short essays to accompany them, now known as the prophecies or 'Judgements'. In fact, the hexagrams and their Judgements alone, form the *I Ching* proper. Everything else is commentary or explanation of the Judgements.

Some time in the next 60 years, King Wen's son, the Duke of Chou, composed the Lines. These were his interpretations of the meanings of the individual broken or solid lines, within the context of each hexagram. He interpreted the meanings of all 384 lines, keeping within the general meanings of the hexagrams as interpreted by his father. In this way, he carried on his father's work, by expanding the divinatory possibilities of the hexagrams.

For the next 600 years, the Chinese used the *I Ching* as an oracle and an aid to divination. Confucius himself was greatly influenced by the book, and much of what we know today as Confucianism is based on it, as is much of Taoism. Towards the end of his life, Confucius decided to add his own comments to the book. In 483 BC, he wrote his celebrated 'Commentaries' and 'Symbolisms' to the *I Ching*. The Commentaries are his remarks on the Judgements of King Wen; the Symbolisms, his remarks on the Lines of the Duke of Chou.

Throughout the centuries, thousands of scholars have tried to interpret the *I Ching*. One of the most significant contributors to the translation of the book was Richard Wilhelm; another was the nineteenth-century Sinologist James Legge. The latter's approach was different from that of his predecessors in that, whereas earlier translators had mainly translated word for word from the Chinese, Legge realised that the individual characters in the Chinese language do not translate as words, but rather as complete ideas or concepts. He was able to render the *I Ching* into the classic version that we know today, in which the readings closely approximate to the original ideas of the authors.

THE 64 HEXAGRAMS

1	2	3	4
Ch'ien	K'un	Chun	Meng

5	6	7	8
Hsu	Sung	Shih	Pi

9	10	11	12
Hsaio Ch'u	Lu	T'ai	P'i

13	14	15	16
T'ung Jen	Ta Yu	Ch'ien	Yu

17	18	19	20
Sui	Ku	Lin	Kuan

21	22	23	24
Shih Ho	Pi	Po	Fu

25	26	27	28
Wu Wang	Ta Ch'u	I	Ta Kuo

29	30	31	32
K'an	Li	Hsien	Heng

33	34	35	36
Tun	Ta Chuang	Chin	Ming I

37	38	39	40
Chia Jen	K'uei	Chien	Chieh

41	42	43	44
Sun	I	Kuai	Kou

45	46	47	48
Ts'ui	Sheng	K'un	Ching

49	50	51	52
Ko	Ting	Chen	Ken

53	54	55	56
Chien	Kuei Mei	Feng	Lu

57	58	59	60
Sun	Tui	Huan	Chieh

61	62	63	64
Chung Fu	Hsaio Kuo	Chi Chi	Wei Chi

Religion and the I Ching

To understand the nature of the *I Ching,* it is necessary to have some idea of the world at the time of its writing. In the twelfth century BC, Chinese life had for centuries been of a feudal nature. Rival warlords fought among themselves, each commanding the loyalties of their subjects. China was an isolated society, mostly due to the fact that its people were constantly warring with each other. Consequently, little influence entered China from the outside world.

China was then one of the oldest civilisations in the world. Only in the Mediterranean area was there any other semblance of structured civilisation. Egypt had been flourishing for centuries and was now in decline. Minoan and Hittite civilisations had grown and died. Phoenician civilisation was growing and was trading with Egypt. Greek civilisation was in the process of being formed.

A century previously, the Egyptian oppression of the Israelites had begun under Rameses II and the Israelites had been led out of Egypt by Moses, subsequently to invade Palestine under the leadership of Joshua.

Many different deities were worshipped throughout the world, although it may be true to say that only Egypt had any form of state-organised religion, and this was probably brought about by the pharaohs solely as a measure of self-preservation. A far older religion existed and was practised by the Israelites. It was the world's first great monotheist religion, Judaism. Although Judaism in its basic form had been practised by the Jews since the birth of their race, it only took an organised and positive form when Moses led the Jewish tribes out of Egypt and presented them with the Ten Commandments.

This was in approximately 1230 BC, 87 years before King Wen devised the hexagrams and wrote his Judgements. Any connection between the imposition of the law of Moses and the composition of the *I Ching* can only be guessed at. The two civilisations were, for various reasons, unlikely to have had dealings with one another. There is no evidence to show that the two peoples were even aware of each other's existence. The Jews were busy building a new home for themselves and the Chinese were engaged in the battles that accompanied the change from one dynasty to another. The nature of Judaism, in that one is *born* a Jew, meant it was unlikely that the Jews would have travelled elsewhere to convert others.

Having said that, the fact remains that the basic principles of the Ten Commandments are uncannily similar to the Judgements in the *I Ching*. In the former, the Jews were told that they should not kill, commit adultery, bear false witness, commit idolatory, steal or covet their neighbours' wives or goods. By comparison, the Judgements of the *I Ching* are full of similar advice.

How then did the Judgements of King Wen and the Lines of his son, the Duke of Chou, so closely resemble the code of behaviour imposed by Moses on the Jews? Perhaps there existed at that time a universal belief in the difference between right and wrong, but that is rather doubtful. Certainly, every society develops omens and beliefs and they could be expected to be especially popular in times of war. Omen tablets have been discovered which date back to Babylonian culture in 2000 BC, and it is possible that some Babylonian omens could have found their way into Chinese life. The Babylonians, however, were not renowned for their good behaviour and so it is unlikely that their omens had any influence on the formation of the *I Ching*.

There is some evidence to suggest that the Chinese themselves had developed their society along the lines of decent and correct behaviour. Rather than a result of religious teaching, this could have developed as a result of a collective 'greenhouse' mentality – not doing unto others, in case they do it to you. This would also contain the necessary binding ingredient – fear. Individuals in a religious society may have refrained from certain behaviour for fear of retribution in the next world; the Chinese may simply have feared the same in this.

The Chinese had long believed in the mystical properties of nature. They observed cyclic change in the passing of the seasons and applied this to human behaviour. They also believed in the oneness of the universe, that everything was intimately interconnected. If a person were to move an arm to the right, it was their belief that the entire universe would move with it. From this came their belief in the common good. Good behaviour towards one person had the effect of adding to the good of society as a whole. A parallel can be drawn with the words spoken by Christ a thousand years later when He said that whatsoever was done for the least of His brethren was done also for Him.

Also significant is the relationship between the teachings of Buddha and the contribution of Confucius to the *I Ching*. There is no apparent evidence to indicate that the cultures from which the two men came ever had any dealings with one another. Nevertheless, the men were certainly contemporaries. The Buddha died in 480 BC; Confucius died the year after, 479 BC. This is a significant coincidence.

So, we are still none the wiser. Was the compilation of the *I Ching* affected by outside influences, or was it purely the product of Chinese philosophy at that time? The religious believer, regardless of creed, may perhaps see it as significant that the *I Ching* was written at approximately the same time as the handing-down of the Ten Commandments and may ascribe its writing to God's desire to get His message across to a different culture. This is more likely, perhaps, than a selective deity – one who would choose a single race alone to follow His teaching and to have an afterlife. All of the world's major religions can be seen to have the same basic ground rules, with cosmetic differences designed to appeal to varying national temperaments.

Maybe the *I Ching* was God's method of instructing the Chinese. Today, whereas Christians and Jews read the Bible, and Moslems the Koran, the Chinese consult the *I Ching*. Perhaps the Westerner, with faith in a universal spirit, may also obtain spiritual benefit from the study of the *I Ching*. Certainly, no harm can come from looking to improve your behaviour towards others.

The Function of the I Ching

The *I Ching* encourages meditation by providing self-knowledge and a greater awareness of the world and our relationship to it. It has been described as a comprehensive method of viewing the world and the universe as an organised whole. It creates order out of chaos. It also foretells the future. This latter idea is based upon the Chinese belief that the future develops in accordance with fixed laws and according to calculable numbers. If these numbers are known, future events can be calculated with absolute certainty.

The *I Ching* has a personality of its own and must be approached with respect. An open mind and a willingness to learn are both essential. The *I Ching* is the result of the combined wisdom of the most respected Chinese sages, and its pronouncements should therefore be treated with a certain respect. Remember that the ancient authors of the book thought in a different way from us today, partly due to the then different structure of society and partly due to the underlying differences between Eastern and Western thought and education.

The *I Ching* is an aid to meditation. You should first meditate upon your question and then upon the answer arrived at through the formation of the hexagrams (see page 24). The *I Ching* will not tell you what is going to happen, but it will direct your attention to alternatives. The answers show the probable consequences of choosing one path rather than another.

The Reason Behind the New I Ching

U ntil recently, the *I Ching* as we know it in the West was the result both of Richard Wilhelm's definitive work and James Legge's brilliant translation in the nineteenth century. Legge's contribution, already mentioned, was a much clearer translation than any of his predecessors, but there were still obstacles in his translation to anyone wishing to understand the oracle. The greatest of these was that the reader, once he or she had formed a hexagram, had to look in ten different places in order to put together an answer.

In his edition of the Legge translation, in 1971, Raymond Van Over painstakingly combined many of Legge's appendices. As a result, the Judgement, Commentary, Symbolism and Lines could all be found under the heading of the relevant hexagram. Without Van Over's arrangement of the text, this new version would have taken many more years to prepare and would perhaps not have been as accurate as it is.

I first encountered the *I Ching* in 1983 and found it to be a remarkable aid to decision-making. I had always regarded myself as a rather indecisive person, but as I became more and more interested in the answers I obtained from the use of the *I Ching*, I found my indecisiveness disappearing. The book didn't actually make decisions for me, but helped me to make them for myself by pointing out the logic of different actions, together with the possible outcomes.

Like many people before me, however, I became frustrated by the obscure symbolism of the text. The antics of princes, tigers and geese seemed to have no relevance to everyday modern life. Try as I might, I could find no more than a passing reference to the questions I asked. Initially, I tried to find fixed meanings for the key phrases that recur throughout the book, but I failed to find any consistency. I realised that the phrases drew their meanings from the context of the hexagrams in which they were used. There was, therefore, no short cut to developing an overall understanding of the book. I was left with interpreting the answers as they occurred. I felt that accuracy was lost by the natural tendency to allow wishful thinking or personal fears to colour interpretations of the text.

I decided to rewrite the *I Ching*, using language that was relevant to the present day. I was also determined not to change the original meaning of the text as had happened in several modern versions I had read. Neither did I want to replace the ideas of the original authors with my own. As I progressed with my work, I became encouraged by each step I took. Where one word would suffice instead of three or four, I used it. The result is a clarified and simplified text. In particular, my translation of the Lines uses economy of words, encouraging the reader to use them as a catalyst for personal intuition.

For example, the text of the Judgement in the Legge translation for Hexagram 48, CHING (A Well), is as follows:

JUDGEMENT – Looking at Ching, we think of how the site of a town may be changed, while the fashion of its walls undergoes no change. The water of a well never disappears and never receives any great increase, and those who come and those who go, can draw and enjoy the benefit. If the drawing has nearly been accomplished, but, before the rope has quite reached the water, the bucket has broken, this is evil.

My version of the Judgement is as follows:

JUDGEMENT – Ching represents mutual helpfulness, as symbolised by the unchanging nature of a well, the value of which depends on the water being extracted from it.

The second version is simpler and easier to understand, and shows the meaning of the hexagram more plainly. None of the original meaning has been lost. My greatest difficulty came with translating the Lines. The original Lines, as composed by the Duke of Chou, sometimes strayed from the context of the hexagrams to which they related. I therefore aimed to bring them within the context of their appropriate hexagrams, while leaving them basically unchanged from their original individual meanings. For example, this Line from Hexagram 50, TING (The Cauldron) reads as follows in the original:

9 in the 2nd place. The second line, undivided, shows the cauldron with the things to be cooked in it. If its subject can say 'My enemy dislikes me, but he cannot approach me,' there will be good fortune.

My version of the Line is as follows:

9 in the 2nd place. Caution will give enemies nothing to point at.

Again, the second version is much simpler to understand; it doesn't waste words and the original meaning has not been lost. The text still requires meditation, but this is made easier by the simplified wording.

How To Consult the New I Ching

n order to consult the *New I Ching,* one must first have a question in mind. The best type of question is a direct one such as, 'Should I do this thing at this time?' or 'Will my meeting with this person be successful tomorrow?' You should write the question on a piece of paper to help to keep it firmly in your mind. You will then need to create a hexagram and obtain a reading from the *I Ching,* which should help you to answer your question.

THE HEXAGRAM

A hexagram is created by throwing yarrow stalks or by tossing three coins. Its form is therefore dictated by the laws of chance. The yarrow stalks may have a feeling of ritual about them, but tossing the coins is simpler and less time consuming. For these reasons, only the latter option is explained here.

THROWING THE COINS

The denomination of the coins used is unimportant, although it is better if they are of the same denomination. Heads are usually used to represent Yang; tails to represent Yin. Each head thrown counts as 3, each tail as 2.

The coins should be thrown by placing them in cupped hands, shaking them and then dropping them over the middle of a table, so that they do not roll off. The value of the three coins thrown is then added up and one of four lines is drawn as shown on the next page.

THE LINES

Coins show	Score	Represented by
3 TAILS	6 (moving line)	——x——
2 TAILS, 1 HEAD	7 (young Yang)	————
1 TAIL, 2 HEADS	8 (young Yin)	—— ——
3 HEADS	9 (moving line)	——●——

FORMING A HEXAGRAM

A hexagram is constructed by throwing the three coins six times. The first line is used as the base of the hexagram and the subsequent lines are drawn above it. The hexagram should be drawn below the written question. Here is an example of a hexagram being constructed.

1st throw
One tail and two heads.
This scores 8. We write:

2nd throw
Three heads.
This scores 9. We write:

3rd throw
One tail and two heads.
This scores 8. We write:

4th throw
One tail and two heads.
This scores 8. We write:

5th throw
Two tails and one head.
This scores 7. We write:

6th throw
Three tails.
This scores 6. We write:

MOVING LINES

The lines created by throwing three tails or three heads are called moving lines as it is in their nature to reverse their polarity. The broken line of a moving 6 (——X——) will change to a solid line (————————), while the solid line of a moving 9 (——●——) will change to a broken line (—— ——).

The hexagram formed in our example will therefore change.

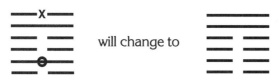

will change to

The new hexagram should now be written next to the original one on the piece of paper. Some hexagrams, of course, will not contain any moving lines and therefore will not change.

CONSULTING THE KEY

You should now consult the Key to the Hexagrams on page 28. This requires you to see your hexagram as two trigrams: the upper (top three lines) and lower (bottom three lines). If there are moving lines in your original hexagram, you will need to find the number for both of the hexagrams that you have constructed.

In our example, the first hexagram formed is number 29 and the second is number 20.

You should now turn to the list of hexagrams, which starts on page 29, and look up the number (or numbers) that you found in the key.

In our example, number 29 is K'AN (Perilous Pit) and number 20 is KUAN (Contemplation).

29 – K'AN
(Perilous Pit)

20 – KUAN
(Contemplation)

OBTAINING THE READINGS

If there were no moving lines in your original hexagram, and you therefore have only one hexagram number, you should read only the text: the Judgement, the Commentary and the Symbolism.

If, however, there were moving lines, you should read the relevant Lines of your first hexagram, and the text of both the first and second hexagrams.

In our example, you would read the following from Hexagram 29:

9 in the 2nd place	Although danger is unavoidable, it will not increase.
6 at the top	Inability to get out of danger, even at its height, will lead to harm.
JUDGEMENT	K'an represents danger, and how to get out of it. Worthy action by those who aim to do the right thing will be valuable.
COMMENTARY	K'an indicates the wisdom of knowing when to act and when not to act. Decency will succeed in the face of danger.
SYMBOLISM	K'an symbolises the need to hold on to virtues, so that danger can be dealt with whenever it may occur.

And the following from Hexagram 20:

JUDGEMENT   Kuan represents the way we should
                       appear to others – sincere and dignified.

COMMENTARY   Kuan indicates how those in authority
                       should be respected.

SYMBOLISM   Kuan symbolises the sense in seeing
                       what people need before deciding what
                       to do.

You should now interpret the readings within the context of your question. The scope of the *I Ching* is huge. The total number of readings, or permutations, that can be obtained with the hexagrams is 64^2, or 4096, a range which is considered sufficient to express all human conditions or situations.

It only remains for me to wish you success in your relationship with the *New I Ching*. As in all things, practice and perseverance will enhance and increase knowledge of the book and will open up a greater understanding of the wealth of advice in its pages. It is this thought process that will lead to personal development.

Key to the Hexagrams

Upper Trigram → Lower Trigram ↓	☰	☳	☵	☶	☷	☴	☲	☱
☰	1	34	5	26	11	9	14	43
☳	25	51	3	27	24	42	21	17
☵	6	40	29	4	7	59	64	47
☶	33	62	39	52	15	53	56	31
☷	12	16	8	23	2	20	35	45
☴	44	32	48	18	46	57	50	28
☲	13	55	63	22	36	37	30	49
☱	10	54	60	41	19	61	38	58

The Hexagrams

CH'IEN

CREATIVE

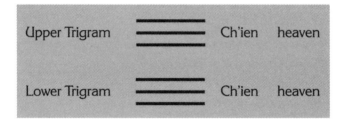

Upper Trigram	Ch'ien	heaven
Lower Trigram	Ch'ien	heaven

JUDGEMENT   Ch'ien represents originality, correctness and gain.

COMMENTARY   Ch'ien indicates cause and effect. Dignity and wisdom are also indicated. Change and transformation are called for, to preserve harmony.

SYMBOLISM   Ch'ien symbolises strength; also renewal and change as seen in the revolving of the heavens. The subject should be constantly active.

LINES – CH'IEN

9 in the 1st place
It is not the time for action.

9 in the 2nd place
It is time to appear and make
oneself known.

9 in the 3rd place
The proper path must be followed,
day and night.

9 in the 4th place
There will be no harm in moving
forward now.

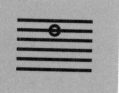

9 in the 5th place
It is time to set to work.

9 at the top
Choose to be humble and modest,
rather than complacent.

K'UN
—————————— *RECEPTIVE* ——————————

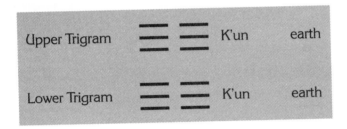

| Upper Trigram | K'un | earth |
| Lower Trigram | K'un | earth |

JUDGEMENT   K'un represents originality, correctness and gain, through obedience and willingness to learn. The person should not take the initiative, but should follow, and should find others with similar opinions and principles to follow alongside. Quietness will bring good fortune.

COMMENTARY   While Ch'ien is the source of all things, K'un gives them life. Quietness will bring great results.

SYMBOLISM   K'un symbolises the capacity and sustaining power of the earth.

LINES – K'UN

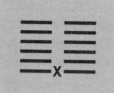

6 in the 1st place
The ice is too thin; wait for it to thicken.

6 in the 2nd place
A balanced approach will lead to gain.

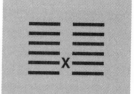

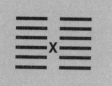

6 in the 3rd place
Excellence should be continued, but hidden.

6 in the 4th place
Through carefulness, no blame or injury will occur.

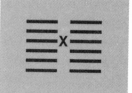

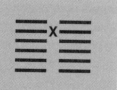

6 in the 5th place
Correctness and humility will bring good fortune and honour.

6 at the top
Do not be too submissive, or others may take advantage of you.

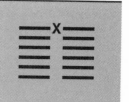

CHUN
—INITIAL DIFFICULTY—

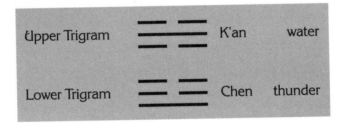

| Upper Trigram | | K'an | water |
| Lower Trigram | | Chen | thunder |

JUDGEMENT Chun represents progress and success, after initial difficulties. Caution must be exercised before action. Advantage will come from sustained appropriate behaviour, and from delegating duties to those who are able.

COMMENTARY Chun indicates moving in areas of danger, which requires skill and wisdom. Delegation should not breed indifference.

SYMBOLISM Chun symbolises the end of oppression.

LINES – CHUN

9 in the 1st place
Despite initial difficulty,
perseverance and humility will
finally triumph.

6 in the 2nd place
Although difficulties continue,
remaining firm will bring success.

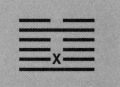

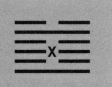

6 in the 3rd place
The person remains firm, realising
that unguided progress brings
regret.

6 in the 4th place
Once help has been found,
moving on will bring benefits.

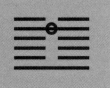

9 in the 5th place
Good fortune will come from
attempting great things now.

6 at the top
At the height of danger lies retreat
and failure.

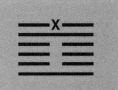

MENG
—YOUTHFUL INEXPERIENCE—

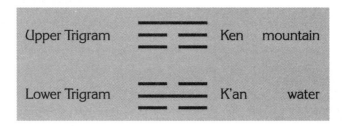

| Upper Trigram | | Ken | mountain |
| Lower Trigram | | K'an | water |

JUDGEMENT

Meng represents youth and inexperience and the method of dealing with it by the experienced elder. The teacher does not look for the pupil; it is the pupil who looks for knowledge. When the pupil opens his or her mind, the teacher fills it and there will be progress and success. But if the pupil does not listen, the teacher will no longer instruct.

COMMENTARY

Meng indicates the good sense of looking for instruction where knowledge is lacking, and being receptive to that instruction.

SYMBOLISM

Meng symbolises the passing of knowledge from the old to the growing. Whatever the time of life, there is more growing to do; no matter how much has been learnt, there is still more to learn.

LINES – MENG

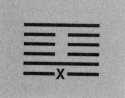

6 in the 1st place
Punishment is a short-term step
for removing ignorance.

9 in the 2nd place
The good teacher exercises
patience and humility, learning
even from the most ignorant.

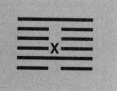

6 in the 3rd place
A person of youth and
inexperience should avoid lifelong
commitment.

6 in the 4th place
No good can arise from stubborn
ignorance.

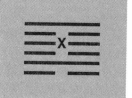

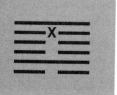

6 in the 5th place
Good fortune will come from a
willingness to learn.

9 at the top
All do, or are done to, according to
their nature.

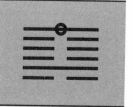

HSU

WAITING

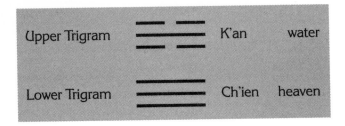

Upper Trigram		K'an	water
Lower Trigram		Ch'ien	heaven

JUDGEMENT   Hsu represents the sense of waiting until success is certain before undertaking anything hazardous. Through waiting will come success.

COMMENTARY   Hsu indicates the sense of overcoming impulsiveness.

SYMBOLISM   Hsu symbolises the virtue of patience. The subject should remain occupied while waiting for the right time to come.

LINES – HSU

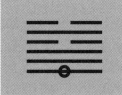

9 in the 1st place
Normal life should be led until the
time is right.

9 in the 2nd place
Sudden action should not be
brought about by insults.

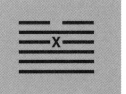

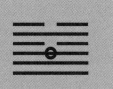

9 in the 3rd place
Hasty action will bring failure.

6 in the 4th place
In dangerous situations, lack of
preparation calls for retreat.

9 in the 5th place
Patience after triumph brings
further triumph.

6 at the top
Help that was not asked for, but
which was gratefully received, will
guarantee success.

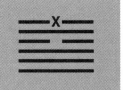

SUNG
———————————CONFLICT———————————

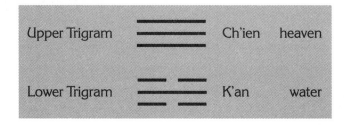

| Upper Trigram | | Ch'ien | heaven |
| Lower Trigram | | K'an | water |

JUDGEMENT   Sung represents opposition and struggle. Through wariness will come good fortune. However, even wariness will not succeed in the face of prolonged struggle. A great enterprise would be rash.

COMMENTARY   Sung indicates the wisdom of changing course in the face of a struggle.

SYMBOLISM   Sung symbolises opposition and contention. Take advice before even entering into a contentious situation.

LINES – SUNG

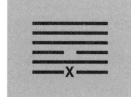

6 in the 1st place
Avoiding dispute may cause others
to mock, but the end will be good.

9 in the 2nd place
When feeling unequal to a
struggle, retreat is called for.

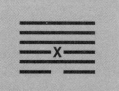

6 in the 3rd place
Staying as you are, or advancing
no more than is necessary, will
bring success.

9 in the 4th place
The realisation that it is right not to
act will lead to good fortune.

9 in the 5th place
Action now will bring great fortune.

9 at the top
Persistence in the face of a
struggle will end in defeat.

SHIH
GROUP ACTION

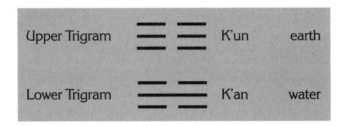

Upper Trigram		K'un	earth
Lower Trigram		K'an	water

JUDGEMENT
Shih represents the presence of good fortune as a result of group action ordered by an experienced person, provided that both the cause and action are right.

COMMENTARY
Shih indicates the willingness of people to follow a trusted leader, even into danger. The cause and effect must, therefore, be right and proper.

SYMBOLISM
Shih symbolises the good fortune that will result from well-intentioned action.

LINES – SHIH

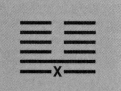

6 in the 1st place
A cause or action that is not right
will lead to failure.

9 in the 2nd place
If confidence is placed in the
leader, there will be good fortune.

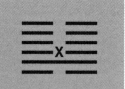

6 in the 3rd place
Divided authority will lead to
failure.

6 in the 4th place
In this situation it is right to retreat.

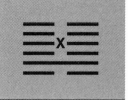

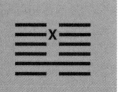

6 in the 5th place
Only defensive actions are right;
only sole leadership will succeed.

6 at the top
Those who are incompetent
should not be allowed to lead
others.

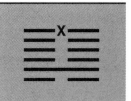

Pi

Union

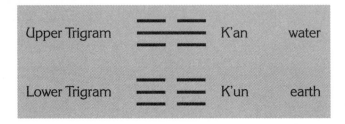

Upper Trigram		K'an	water
Lower Trigram		K'un	earth

JUDGEMENT

Pi represents the idea of union between different types of people. The person who wants others to follow should examine his or her own fitness to lead. If that person is worthy, others will unite as followers and good will come from it, but only if they do not delay.

COMMENTARY

Pi indicates success as a result of individuals coming together willingly to follow a leader. But some do not wish for union until it is too late and this will bring bad luck.

SYMBOLISM

Pi symbolises the tendency to seek complete union.

LINES – PI

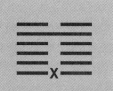

6 in the 1st place
Seeking union will bring other advantages.

6 in the 2nd place
The desire for union stems from good intentions.

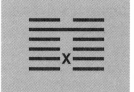

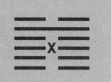

6 in the 3rd place
Seeking union with undesirable people will bring bad luck.

6 in the 4th place
Seeking union with the right person will bring good fortune.

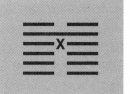

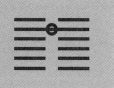

9 in the 5th place
A person who brings about union inspires confidence and trust.

6 at the top
Seeking union when it is too late will lead to bad luck.

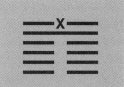

HSAIO CH'U
── TAMING FORCE ──

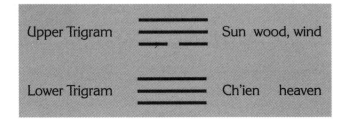

Upper Trigram		Sun wood, wind
Lower Trigram		Ch'ien heaven

JUDGEMENT   Hsaio Ch'u represents restraint in small things. This will lead to progress and success.

COMMENTARY   Hsaio Ch'u indicates that exercising restraint in small measures will bring success.

SYMBOLISM   Hsaio Ch'u symbolises the ability temporarily to restrain. The person should control the outward appearance of virtue.

LINES – HSAIO CH'U

9 in the 1st place
Those with a strong nature will
prosper.

9 in the 2nd place
Doing one's duty will bring good
fortune.

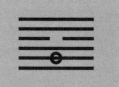

9 in the 3rd place
Lack of restraint will bring bad
luck.

6 in the 4th place
Apprehension is misplaced in the
restraint of others.

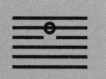

9 in the 5th place
The sincere person unites others
in a common cause.

9 at the top
Continue to exercise restraint,
or risk harm.

LU

—TREADING CAREFULLY—

Upper Trigram	☰	Ch'ien	heaven
Lower Trigram	☱	Tui	marsh, lake

JUDGEMENT   Lu represents success, brought about by treading carefully through life.

COMMENTARY   Lu indicates weakness triumphing over strength, through caution.

SYMBOLISM   Lu symbolises the wisdom of being aware of the proper place of different people in the scheme of things.

LINES – LU

9 in the 1st place
With the right intentions,
proceeding with confidence will
lead to no harm.

9 in the 2nd place
The quiet person takes the steady
path to good fortune.

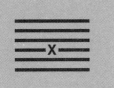

6 in the 3rd place
To advance with more ability in
mind than in fact will lead to
disaster.

9 in the 4th place
Awareness of danger will bring
caution and lead to good fortune.

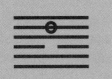

9 in the 5th place
The higher one is raised up, the
further one will fall.

9 at the top
If every step has been right, the
result will be good.

T'AI

──────── PEACE ────────

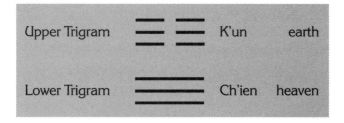

Upper Trigram　　　　　K'un　　earth

Lower Trigram　　　　　Ch'ien　heaven

JUDGEMENT　　T'ai represents the growth of peace between opposing factors and the good fortune that results.

COMMENTARY　T'ai indicates the peaceful union of the strong with the weak. The person should mix with others.

SYMBOLISM　　T'ai symbolises the way in which the giver ensures that everyone can receive their gifts easily.

LINES – T'AI

9 in the 1st place
Determination to proceed will
bring good luck.

9 in the 2nd place
Through adaptation will come
peaceful enjoyment of strength.

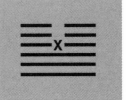

9 in the 3rd place
Realisation of the changing nature
of things will bring peace.

6 in the 4th place
Help that is not looked for will be
given freely and willingly.

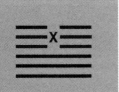

6 in the 5th place
Correct action will lead to great
success.

6 at the top
Continued failure to defend
oneself will end in defeat.

P'I

Stagnation

Upper Trigram		Ch'ien	heaven
Lower Trigram		K'un	earth

JUDGEMENT

P'i represents stagnation and decay after growth has finished. Failure to understand others will lead to bad luck.

COMMENTARY

P'i indicates the necessity of those in authority taking the initiative.

SYMBOLISM

P'i symbolises avoiding disaster by concealing virtues.

LINES – P'I

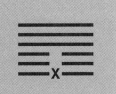

6 in the 1st place
Open-mindedness will encourage
loyalty.

6 in the 2nd place
Patience and obedience will
resolve problems successfully.

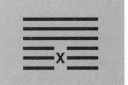

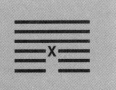

6 in the 3rd place
Merely contemplating doing the
wrong thing will bring feelings of
shame.

9 in the 4th place
Action that is ordered by heaven
will be successful.

9 in the 5th place
Caution is needed, even in the
midst of success.

9 at the top
Even the worst distress must
change to good fortune.

T'UNG JEN
COMPANIONSHIP

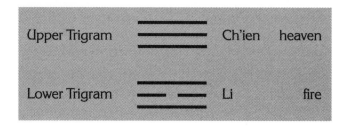

| Upper Trigram | | Ch'ien | heaven |
| Lower Trigram | | Li | fire |

JUDGEMENT   T'ung Jen represents the virtue of unselfish union or companionship. The greatest difficulties will be dealt with, resulting in progress and success. The person should remember to act correctly at all times.

COMMENTARY   T'ung Jen indicates intelligence supported by strength of character.

SYMBOLISM   T'ung Jen symbolises the naturalness of wishing for union.

LINES – T'UNG JEN

9 in the 1st place
Even the desire for union must
come from unselfishness.

6 in the 2nd place
Union of like with like only is
narrow-minded and will lead to
regret.

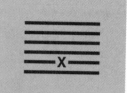

9 in the 3rd place
The weaker person avoids union
with the stronger, which would
bring bad luck.

9 in the 4th place
Caution and right-mindedness will
lead to good fortune.

9 in the 5th place
The person who wants union will
overcome obstacles and achieve
their desire.

9 at the top
Although union is only partly
achieved, there will be no harm
done.

TA YU

———————ABUNDANCE———————

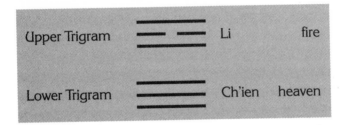

Upper Trigram   Li   fire

Lower Trigram   Ch'ien   heaven

JUDGEMENT   Ta Yu represents a state of prosperity.

COMMENTARY   Ta Yu indicates strength directed by intelligence and the benefits of acting at the proper time.

SYMBOLISM   Ta Yu symbolises the wisdom of always distinguishing between good and evil.

LINES – TA YU

9 in the 1st place
Acting correctly, while bearing difficulties in mind, will lead to no harm.

9 in the 2nd place
An abundance of virtues will only bring good in whatever is done.

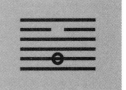

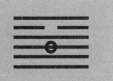

9 in the 3rd place
The undeserving, lacking virtue, will pretend to be superior.

9 in the 4th place
Restraint of power injures no one.

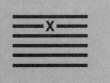

6 in the 5th place
Sincerity concealed by dignity leads to good fortune.

9 at the top
Moderated strength will always bring good fortune.

CH'IEN
MODESTY

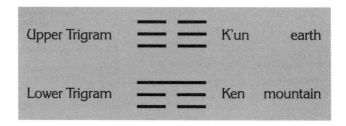

Upper Trigram	K'un	earth
Lower Trigram	Ken	mountain

JUDGEMENT   Ch'ien represents the way to success through modesty.

COMMENTARY   Ch'ien indicates the high value set upon modesty. Those who are modest will be successful.

SYMBOLISM   Ch'ien symbolises the virtue of dealing with everyone on their own level.

LINES – CH'IEN

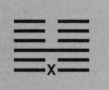

6 in the 1st place
People who see themselves on the same level as others will have good fortune.

6 in the 2nd place
Modesty in action will bring good fortune.

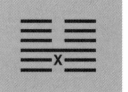

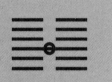

9 in the 3rd place
Modesty in accomplishment will ensure sustained success.

6 in the 4th place
Those who are successful and prosperous should remain modest.

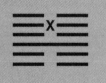

6 in the 5th place
Those who are modest will find that everything they do leads to good.

6 at the top
Those who are modest will be able to see their limitations.

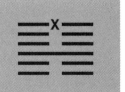

yu

——————————— HARMONY ———————————

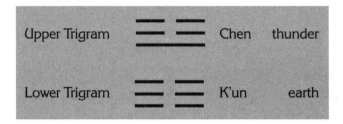

Upper Trigram		Chen	thunder
Lower Trigram		K'un	earth

JUDGEMENT   Yu represents a state of harmony and contentment.

COMMENTARY   Yu indicates how contentment moves people to obedience.

SYMBOLISM   Yu symbolises the joy that is felt after problems have been resolved.

LINES – YU

6 in the 1st place
Drawing attention to one's own pleasure will bring cause for regret.

6 in the 2nd place
The honest person who also has foresight will be successful.

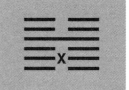

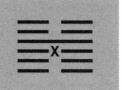

6 in the 3rd place
Laziness and the pursuit of pleasure will lead to no good.

9 in the 4th place
The person who creates and maintains harmony will enjoy sustained success.

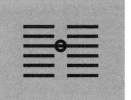

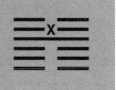

6 in the 5th place
Weakness allows pleasure to gain control, but not indefinitely.

6 at the top
Even the weakest-willed will survive, if they choose to change.

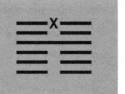

SUI

FOLLOWING

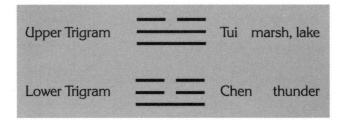

| Upper Trigram | Tui | marsh, lake |
| Lower Trigram | Chen | thunder |

JUDGEMENT Sui represents the idea of following. Where everything is as it should be, there will unmistakably be great progress and success.

COMMENTARY Sui indicates respecting those in authority.

SYMBOLISM Sui symbolises how action is always followed by reaction.

LINES – SUI

9 in the 1st place
Unselfish and right-minded changing of course will bring a deserved reward.

6 in the 2nd place
The following of inexperience leaves no room for the gaining of experience.

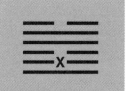

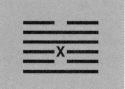

6 in the 3rd place
Those who follow experience, rather than inexperience, will find what they are looking for.

9 in the 4th place
Those who are followed can only avoid harm through sincere loyalty.

9 in the 5th place
The true seeking of excellence will bring success.

6 at the top
Only what is right must be followed.

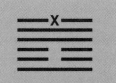

KU

―――――――― STOPPING DECAY ―――――――――

| Upper Trigram | Ken | mountain |
| Lower Trigram | Sun | wood, wind |

JUDGEMENT Ku represents the stopping of decay and a return to good condition. Great efforts will be required to achieve this, but great progress and success will result.

COMMENTARY Ku indicates the creation of order out of chaos.

SYMBOLISM Ku symbolises disorder. Helping people will be a saving virtue.

LINES – KU

6 in the 1st place
Concealing the blame of others
will lead to good fortune.

9 in the 2nd place
Gentle correction will lead to good.

9 in the 3rd place
Surrendering in the face of
excesses will cause no harm.

6 in the 4th place
Indulgence will lead to failure.

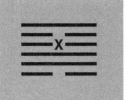

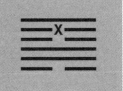

6 in the 5th place
Correct behaviour will bring praise.

9 at the top
On this occasion it is best not to
take part.

LIɅ

APPROACH

Upper Trigram	☷	K'un	earth
Lower Trigram	☱	Tui	marsh, lake

JUDGEMENT   Lin represents the approach of authority. Appropriate behaviour will bring great progress and success. Remember, however, that the authority will not always be there.

COMMENTARY   Lin indicates strength, leading to pleasure and agreement.

SYMBOLISM   Lin symbolises the approach made by those in authority, as they look for the support of their followers.

LINES – LIN

9 in the 1st place
The intention to do right will bring success.

9 in the 2nd place
Going forward now will bring results.

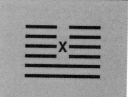

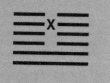

6 in the 3rd place
Willingness to go forward in these circumstances will lead to no good, but caution will improve matters.

6 in the 4th place
Advancing with the highest intentions will lead to no harm.

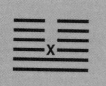

6 in the 5th place
Authority with wisdom will bring good fortune.

6 at the top
Honesty and generosity will lead to success.

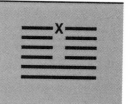

KUAN

CONTEMPLATION

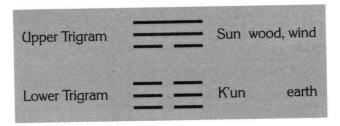

Upper Trigram		Sun	wood, wind
Lower Trigram		K'un	earth

JUDGEMENT   Kuan represents the way we should appear to others – sincere and dignified.

COMMENTARY   Kuan indicates how those in authority should be respected.

SYMBOLISM   Kuan symbolises the sense in seeing what people need before deciding what to do.

LINES – KUAN

6 in the 1st place
Thoughtlessness and near-sightedness are both examples of inferior behaviour.

6 in the 2nd place
Those in authority should not be reticent or timid.

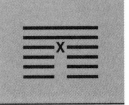

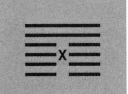

6 in the 3rd place
Flexibility will bring about action only at the proper time.

6 in the 4th place
Contemplation of the achievements of others will give birth to ambition.

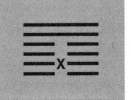

9 in the 5th place
Self-examination and unselfish consideration will do no harm.

9 at the top
Contemplation of one's own character will lead to improvement.

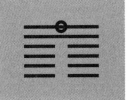

SHIH HO
BITING THROUGH

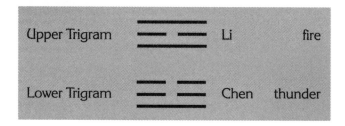

Upper Trigram		Li	fire
Lower Trigram		Chen	thunder

JUDGEMENT Shih Ho represents the wisdom of removing obstacles to union, so that all people may come together unhindered.

COMMENTARY Shih Ho indicates lenient judgement.

SYMBOLISM Shih Ho symbolises the bringing together of dignity and intelligence in the forming of judgements.

LINES – SHIH HO

9 in the 1st place
Those who are punished may be
deterred from doing wrong again.

6 in the 2nd place
Effective action must be continued
and increased, until the effect is
achieved.

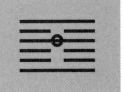

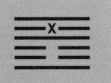

6 in the 3rd place
It may be unpleasant to punish
others, but no great harm will be
done.

9 in the 4th place
Judgement based on strength and
caution will bring good fortune.

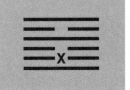

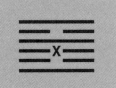

6 in the 5th place
Leniency in judgement will lead to
no wrong.

9 at the top
Those who fall back into wrong-
doing may hear, but do not listen;
this leads to harm.

Pl

ADORNMENT

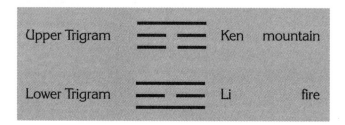

| Upper Trigram | Ken | mountain |
| Lower Trigram | Li | fire |

JUDGEMENT   Pi represents adornment. It must be remembered, however, that adornment is secondary to what is real.

COMMENTARY   Pi indicates the necessity of keeping adornment in check, while remembering what is real.

SYMBOLISM   Pi symbolises appearances enhanced by adornment. In matters of truth, however, it must not be used.

LINES – PI

9 in the 1st place
Adornment is not considered
essential for a good life.

6 in the 2nd place
Adornment is controlled by what is
beneath it.

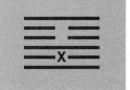

9 in the 3rd place
Decency will bring the respect of
others.

6 in the 4th place
That which is real is recognised as
superior to decoration.

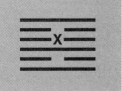

6 in the 5th place
Preference for simplicity and
economy will bring good fortune.

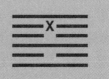

9 at the top
Those who do not choose to
adorn themselves will achieve their
aim.

PO

FALLING APART

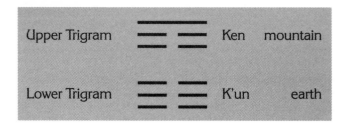

Upper Trigram		Ken	mountain
Lower Trigram		K'un	earth

JUDGEMENT

Po represents the process of falling apart, or overthrowing. There is no advantage in taking any action.

COMMENTARY

Po indicates a temporary defeat of plans. Circumstances are certain to change for the better.

SYMBOLISM

Po symbolises the strengthening of foundations in order to secure the well-being and stability of the higher levels.

LINES – PO

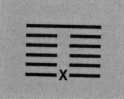

6 in the 1st place
Attempts to overthrow what is right
will lead to evil.

6 in the 2nd place
No good will come of
overthrowing that which is right.

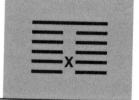

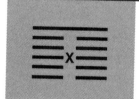

6 in the 3rd place
If the motives to cause change are
good, then no harm will come.

6 in the 4th place
Danger awaits those who have
been overthrown.

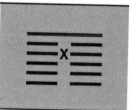

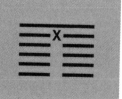

6 in the 5th place
Pleading without motive will lead
to no blame.

9 at the top
Strength survives and gains fresh
strength; there will be no more
danger.

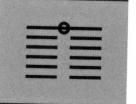

FU

RETURNING

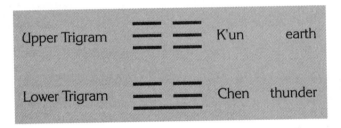

| Upper Trigram | K'un | earth |
| Lower Trigram | Chen | thunder |

JUDGEMENT   Fu represents the idea of returning, or starting again. After decay, things can only improve and any movement will bring good.

COMMENTARY   Fu indicates the naturalness of change and of rejuvenation.

SYMBOLISM   Fu symbolises the return to rest after activity.

LINES – FU

9 in the 1st place
To return, one must first have left the path; there will be great success.

6 in the 2nd place
Returning to the proper path is admirable and will lead to success.

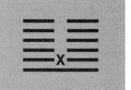

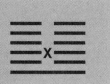

6 in the 3rd place
Repeated returns are dangerous, but this can be avoided by exercising caution.

6 in the 4th place
Compromise will bring about a return to the proper path.

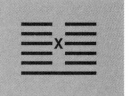

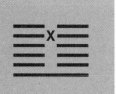

6 in the 5th place
Humble desire for self-improvement will cause no harm.

6 at the top
Returning to the wrong path will lead to disaster.

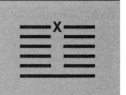

WU WANG
INNOCENCE

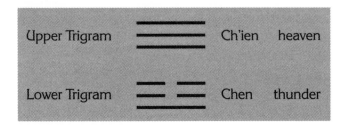

| Upper Trigram | | Ch'ien | heaven |
| Lower Trigram | | Chen | thunder |

JUDGEMENT   Wu Wang represents sincere and careful simplicity. Carelessness will do harm, but consistent correctness will lead to progress and success.

COMMENTARY   Wu Wang indicates the blessed nature of innocence.

SYMBOLISM   Wu Wang symbolises the way in which things are naturally good.

LINES – WU WANG

9 in the 1st place
Sincere action will achieve what is desired.

6 in the 2nd place
Unselfish and good motivation will bring success.

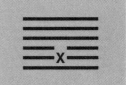

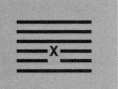

6 in the 3rd place
Innocence will sometimes invite disaster.

9 in the 4th place
Following that which is right will do no harm.

9 in the 5th place
When harm comes to that which is correct, faith will put things right.

9 at the top
Completed actions should be followed by rest; more action would be disastrous.

TA CH'U
―――――――――*TAMING FORCE*―――――――――

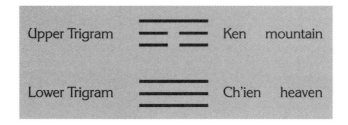

| Upper Trigram | Ken | mountain |
| Lower Trigram | Ch'ien | heaven |

JUDGEMENT   Ta Ch'u represents self-control and growth. Together these will bring strength. Those who want to improve themselves must be right-minded. The most difficult tasks will then end in success.

COMMENTARY   Ta Ch'u indicates a great collection of good qualities, made stronger by restraint. Correct motivation will overcome the strongest opposition. No task will be too great.

SYMBOLISM   Ta Ch'u symbolises the importance of experience and learning in the bringing together of good qualities.

LINES – TA CH'U

9 in the 1st place
To go forward now would lead to
strong opposition.

9 in the 2nd place
There is nothing wrong in holding
back in the face of difficulties.

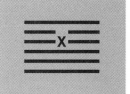

9 in the 3rd place
When in danger, proceeding in any
direction will lead to good.

6 in the 4th place
Looking forward and being
prepared will lead to success.

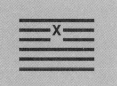

6 in the 5th place
Being prepared will prevent danger
and end in success.

9 at the top
The path to virtue is free; there will
be success.

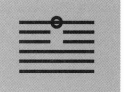

——————————— *NOURISHMENT* ———————————

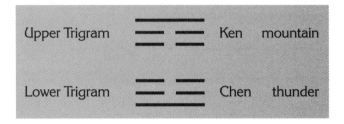

Upper Trigram		Ken	mountain
Lower Trigram		Chen	thunder

JUDGEMENT   I represents the nourishing of the body and mind. The correct motivation is essential for success.

COMMENTARY   I indicates the benefits obtained by nurturing talents and virtues for the greater good of all.

SYMBOLISM   I symbolises the way that moderate eating nourishes the body and moderation in words nourishes the mind.

LINES – I

9 in the 1st place
Lack of effort will lead to bad luck.

6 in the 2nd place
Seeking support from improper
sources will lead to evil.

6 in the 3rd place
Those who believe that they need
nothing from others, when this is
not so, will find that their actions
bring no success.

6 in the 4th place
Looking for support will enable it
to be given; no harm will come.

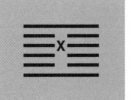

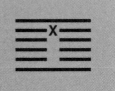

6 in the 5th place
Even when depending on others,
difficult tasks must not be
undertaken.

9 at the top
The tasks of instruction and
support are hard, but there will be
success.

TA KUO

EXCESS

| Upper Trigram | Tui | marsh, lake |
| Lower Trigram | Sun | wood, wind |

JUDGEMENT   Ta Kuo represents the extraordinary measures that are required in extraordinary times. These will bring success.

COMMENTARY   Ta Kuo indicates that some situations call for flexibility in order to achieve success.

SYMBOLISM   Ta Kuo symbolises extraordinary action and events.

LINES – TA KUO

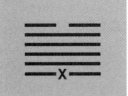

6 in the 1st place
Modesty and carefulness will lead
to no wrong.

9 in the 2nd place
Extraordinary associations may
still bring results.

9 in the 3rd place
The extraordinary strain will be too
great for one alone.

9 in the 4th place
There is enough strength; seeking
help will lead to regret.

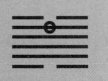

9 in the 5th place
Fruitless associations will soon
decay; there will be neither blame
nor praise.

6 at the top
Attempts to do too much will lead
to disaster, but there will be no
blame.

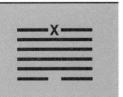

K'AN
PERILOUS PIT

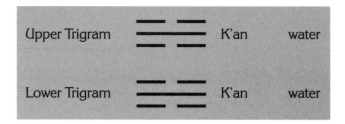

Upper Trigram		K'an	water
Lower Trigram		K'an	water

JUDGEMENT K'an represents danger and how to get out of it. Worthy action by those who aim to do the right thing will be valuable.

COMMENTARY K'an indicates the wisdom of knowing when to act and when not to act. Decency will succeed in the face of danger.

SYMBOLISM K'an symbolises the need to hold on to virtues, so that danger can be dealt with whenever it may occur.

LINES – K'AN

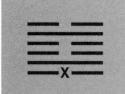

6 in the 1st place
Any action now will only increase the danger.

9 in the 2nd place
Although danger is unavoidable, it will not increase.

6 in the 3rd place
Unproductive movement will not save one from danger.

6 in the 4th place
When unable to prevent danger, no harm will come from asking for help.

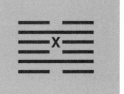

9 in the 5th place
Danger is almost removed; there will be no mistake.

6 at the top
Inability to get out of danger, even at its height, will lead to harm.

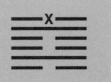

LI

BRIGHTNESS

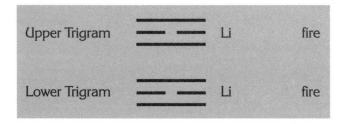

JUDGEMENT   Li represents brightness and intelligence. Modesty attached to intelligence will bring success.

COMMENTARY   Li indicates the fact that everything has its place. Acceptance of this will lead to success.

SYMBOLISM   Li symbolises the development and furthering of intelligence.

LINES – LI

9 in the 1st place
When the way is confused,
carefulness will lead to no harm.

6 in the 2nd place
Sticking to the correct course will
bring success.

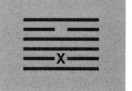

9 in the 3rd place
Unnecessary discontentment will
lead to harm.

9 in the 4th place
Abruptness is unbearable to others
and will lead to disaster.

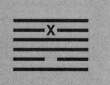

6 in the 5th place
Outward expressions of sadness
show inward modesty; there will be
good fortune.

9 at the top
Great achievements, if they
contain modesty, will do no harm.

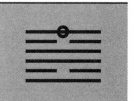

HSIEN
INFLUENCE

Upper Trigram		Tui marsh, lake
Lower Trigram		Ken mountain

JUDGEMENT   Hsien represents the exerting of influence; with the correct intentions, it will lead to good fortune.

COMMENTARY   Hsien indicates how correct influence may bring harmony and peace.

SYMBOLISM   Hsien symbolises the keeping open of the mind to outside influences.

LINES – HSIEN

6 in the 1st place
The wish to influence is useless
without the capability.

6 in the 2nd place
When unable to act without help, it
is better to remain still.

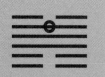

9 in the 3rd place
Exercising influence now will lead
to regret.

9 in the 4th place
Inadequacy calls for the right thing
to be done, if there is to be
success.

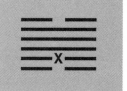

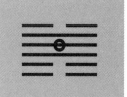

9 in the 5th place
Unselfish influence in trivial
matters will cause no regret.

6 at the top
Empty verbal influence will lead to
no good.

HENG
───────── *PERSEVERANCE* ─────────

Upper Trigram		Chen thunder
Lower Trigram		Sun wood, wind

JUDGEMENT   Heng represents perseverance, leading to progress and success.

COMMENTARY   Heng indicates the ongoing nature of things.

SYMBOLISM   Heng symbolises unchanging activity and steadiness.

LINES – HENG

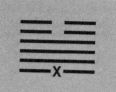

6 in the 1st place
Too early a wish for things to
continue will lead to evil.

9 in the 2nd place
Steadiness will bring no cause for
regret.

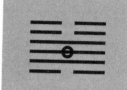

9 in the 3rd place
Failure to maintain virtue will cause
regret.

9 in the 4th place
Continual searching will come to
nothing.

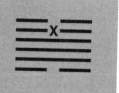

6 in the 5th place
It is correct to persevere with
whatever is right.

6 at the top
Excessive perseverance will lead to
evil.

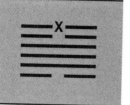

TUN
RETREAT

Upper Trigram	≡	Ch'ien	heaven
Lower Trigram	☶	Ken	mountain

JUDGEMENT

Tun represents the necessity of retreating before those who have the majority. Correct behaviour will lessen the negative effects of this action.

COMMENTARY

Tun indicates that harmful circumstances are best avoided by retreating.

SYMBOLISM

Tun symbolises that even retreat is successful, in that harm does not occur.

LINES – TUN

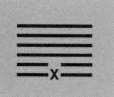

6 in the 1st place
Any movement could bring
trouble; stillness will be safer.

6 in the 2nd place
A firm purpose will not be broken.

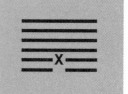

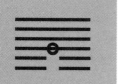

9 in the 3rd place
Those who would stop retreat
should be kept at a distance.

9 in the 4th place
Retreating, despite wishing not to,
will bring success.

9 in the 5th place
Retreating with the correct
motivation will lead to good
fortune.

9 at the top
Retreating with dignity will be
advantageous in every way.

TA CHUANG
―――――――――GREAT POWER―――――――――

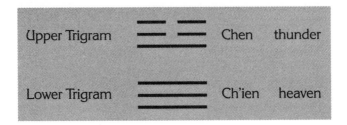

| Upper Trigram | ☳ | Chen | thunder |
| Lower Trigram | ☰ | Ch'ien | heaven |

JUDGEMENT Ta Chuang represents the idea that rightness must conrol strength and work with it in all actions.

COMMENTARY Ta Chuang indicates that great power must be exercised both impartially and unselfishly.

SYMBOLISM Ta Chuang symbolises strength being used to control the self. The person should do the right thing at every step.

LINES – TA CHUANG

9 in the 1st place
Advancing prematurely is exhausting and will certainly bring trouble.

9 in the 2nd place
Strength controlled by the wish to do right will lead to good fortune.

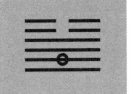

9 in the 3rd place
Cautious use of strength will help to avoid danger.

9 in the 4th place
Advancing with care and the wish to do right will lead to good fortune.

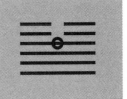

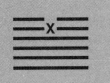

6 in the 5th place
Strength that is controlled and directed will cause no regret.

6 at the top
Resting, due to awareness of weakness, brings good fortune.

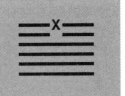

CHIN

PROGRESS

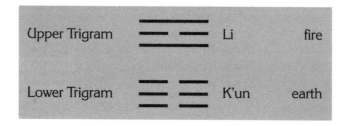

Upper Trigram		Li	fire
Lower Trigram		K'un	earth

JUDGEMENT   Chin represents progress, advance and improvement.

COMMENTARY   Chin indicates advancing and the rewards obtained by doing so.

SYMBOLISM   Chin symbolises the benefits obtained by working to increase one's virtues.

LINES – CHIN

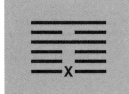

6 in the 1st place
When virtue is unrecognised, it will
be better to advance no further.

6 in the 2nd place
Continuing to advance will bring
good fortune.

6 in the 3rd place
The common aim is to advance;
no harm will come of it.

9 in the 4th place
Secretive advance will lead to
danger.

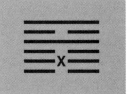

6 in the 5th place
Indifference as to the outcome will
not prevent the advance being
advantageous.

9 at the top
Although using force is
regrettable, the wish to do right will
bring good fortune.

MING I
INTELLIGENCE WOUNDED

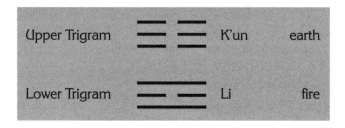

Upper Trigram		K'un	earth
Lower Trigram		Li	fire

JUDGEMENT   Ming I represents repression. It will be useful to recognise repression when it occurs and to maintain one's original aim.

COMMENTARY   Ming I indicates the repression of what is good.

SYMBOLISM   Ming I symbolises the virtue of hiding one's intelligence in the course of one's actions.

LINES – MING I

9 in the 1st place
Those who stop after an initial
setback may be mocked, but a
firm purpose must be maintained.

6 in the 2nd place
An obstacle will not overcome duty
and what is right; there will be
good fortune.

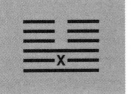

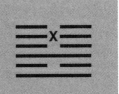

9 in the 3rd place
Success will come, but patience
must be exercised.

6 in the 4th place
Withdrawing from danger now will
cause little damage.

6 in the 5th place
Doing the right thing will help to
prevent total disaster.

6 at the top
Ingratitude will make for less of a
person.

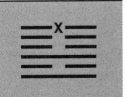

CHIA JEN
FAMILY

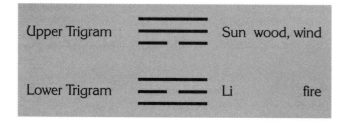

Upper Trigram	☴	Sun wood, wind
Lower Trigram	☲	Li fire

JUDGEMENT   Chia Jen represents the rules of the family, where each member plays his or her own part.

COMMENTARY   Chia Jen indicates that, whereas authority must have force, it must also be gentle.

SYMBOLISM   Chia Jen symbolises the virtue of consistency and doing what is right in the family.

LINES – CHIA JEN

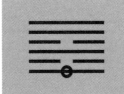

9 in the 1st place
Rules made early on will help to
avoid problems later.

6 in the 2nd place
When members of the family carry
out their duties, there will be good
fortune.

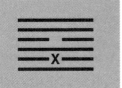

9 in the 3rd place
Strictness, rather than a relaxed
attitude, is more likely to bring
good fortune.

6 in the 4th place
A family ruled by affection and
harmony will have great fortune.

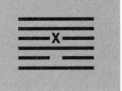

9 in the 5th place
A parent's wish to do the right
thing will be reflected in the family.

9 at the top
The good example of parents to
their children will bring good
fortune.

K'UEI

DIVISION

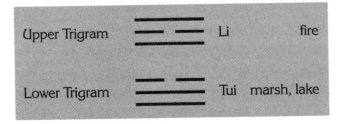

| Upper Trigram | Li | fire |
| Lower Trigram | Tui | marsh, lake |

JUDGEMENT K'uei represents a state of division and how this can be corrected.

COMMENTARY K'uei indicates a state in which separate wills move in different directions.

SYMBOLISM K'uei symbolises the idea of division, even in the midst of general agreement.

LINES – K'UEI

9 in the 1st place
Disappointment will occur unless a
common cause is found.
Goodness may bring success.

9 in the 2nd place
A chance meeting may lead to a
better understanding.

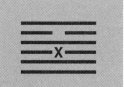

6 in the 3rd place
Whatever is bad now will
eventually become good.

9 in the 4th place
Division giving way to union will
bring success.

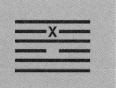

6 in the 5th place
Close and easy union will lead to
success.

9 at the top
Discovering an enemy to be a
friend will bring good fortune.

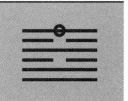

CHIEN
CEASING MOVEMENT

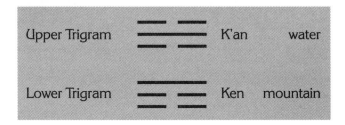

Upper Trigram		K'an	water
Lower Trigram		Ken	mountain

JUDGEMENT
Chien represents various circumstances – some requiring action, others inaction. Whatever the circumstances, the wish to do good is necessary for there to be good fortune.

COMMENTARY
Chien indicates caution in the face of difficulty. When danger is in sight, it is best to advance no further.

SYMBOLISM
Chien symbolises the value of reflection and self-examination when faced with danger or uncertainty.

LINES – CHIEN

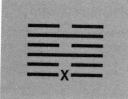

6 in the 1st place
Advancing now will increase difficulties; it will be better to wait for a more favourable time.

6 in the 2nd place
Although unable to cope with difficulties, the wish to do good will bring no blame.

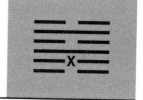

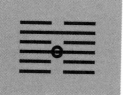

9 in the 3rd place
Moving on without help will be difficult; it is best to wait for a better time.

6 in the 4th place
It is better to unite with one who is stronger and wait until the proper time.

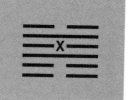

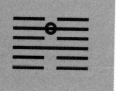

9 in the 5th place
The greatest difficulties can be coped with; friends will help.

6 at the top
There is nowhere to go; good will come from remaining still.

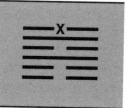

CHIEH
REMOVING OBSTACLES

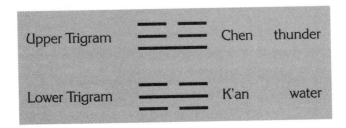

Upper Trigram		Chen	thunder
Lower Trigram		K'an	water

JUDGEMENT Chieh represents removing obstacles and difficulties. When this is done, it is better not to change the old ways. Any action should be taken early to ensure good fortune.

COMMENTARY Chieh indicates the removal of danger.

SYMBOLISM Chieh symbolises the removal of burdens. The person should be gentle and merciful.

LINES – CHIEH

6 in the 1st place
The person will do no wrong.

9 in the 2nd place
Straightforwardness and doing the
right thing will bring success.

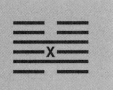

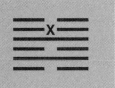

6 in the 3rd place
Obvious vulnerability invites
attack; there will be cause for
regret.

9 in the 4th place
Circumstances are unfavourable;
nothing good will happen.

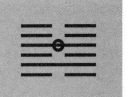

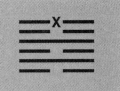

6 in the 5th place
All obstacles have been removed;
there will be good fortune.

6 at the top
Those who aim to do the right
thing will have good fortune.

SUN

—————————— DECREASE ——————————

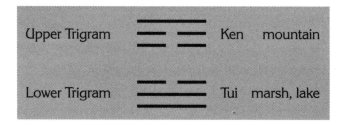

| Upper Trigram | Ken | mountain |
| Lower Trigram | Tui | marsh, lake |

JUDGEMENT   Sun represents decrease. A willing decrease of assets, such as the correct payment of taxes, will bring good fortune.

COMMENTARY   Sun indicates the adjustment of contributions according to the ability to give. No matter how small the contribution, if it is given willingly and sincerely, it will lead to advantage.

SYMBOLISM   Sun symbolises that whatever decreases one thing, increases another.

LINES – SUN

9 in the 1st place
Those who wish to help others should not neglect their own affairs.

9 in the 2nd place
Action will lead to harm; inaction will be more helpful.

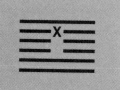

6 in the 3rd place
Many repetitions of thoughts or actions will cause doubts; single-mindedness will bring success.

6 in the 4th place
Difficulties will be lessened by seeking help; there will be no regret.

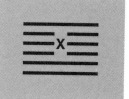

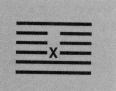

6 in the 5th place
Humbly welcoming help will lead to great good fortune.

9 at the top
Giving to others, without diminishing one's own resources, will bring good fortune.

INCREASE

Upper Trigram		Sun	wood, wind
Lower Trigram		Chen	thunder

JUDGEMENT I represents addition or increase. Movement in any way will lead to gain.

COMMENTARY I indicates unrestricted increase and the pleasure it brings.

SYMBOLISM I symbolises the increasing of what is good and the decreasing of what is bad.

LINES – I

9 in the 1st place
Early movement is rash, but great
success will bring no blame.

6 in the 2nd place
Assets are increased by gifts;
doing the right thing will bring
good fortune.

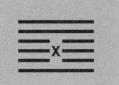

6 in the 3rd place
Adversity will bring out the good
from even the most evil.

6 in the 4th place
Proceeding unselfishly is
acceptable and will bring gain.

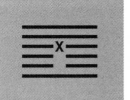

9 in the 5th place
Everyone benefits from the truly
good person; there will certainly be
success.

9 at the top
A selfish concern for increase will
lead to great danger from others.

KUAI

—REMOVING CORRUPTION—

Upper Trigram		Tui marsh, lake
Lower Trigram		Ch'ien heaven

JUDGEMENT Kuai represents the way of dealing with those who do wrong. Those who want to undertake this task must denounce the wrong-doer and inspire the support of others. This should be done as peacefully as possible in order to bring benefits all around.

COMMENTARY Kuai indicates that there must be no selfish motive in the removal of those who do wrong.

SYMBOLISM Kuai symbolises that whatever is accumulated must then be re-dispersed, in the same way that clouds which form from evaporation afterwards turn to rain.

LINES – KUAI

9 in the 1st place
Hasty and unprepared action will lead to failure.

9 in the 2nd place
Honest determination, modified by caution, will protect from harm.

9 in the 3rd place
Those who appear unsure may annoy others, but they will not be blamed.

9 in the 4th place
Solitary action is useless; failure to listen to advice to follow others will lead to no good.

9 in the 5th place
Strength of character will be needed to overcome bad influence, even in the mind.

6 at the top
There is no one to ask for help; bad luck will be the result.

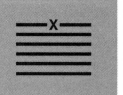

KOU

ENCOUNTERING

Upper Trigram	═══════	Ch'ien heaven
Lower Trigram	═══════	Sun wood, wind

JUDGEMENT   Kou represents suddenly encountering, or casually meeting.

COMMENTARY   Kou indicates the unexpected meeting with blatant boldness.

SYMBOLISM   Kou symbolises the act of reaching everywhere.

LINES - KOU

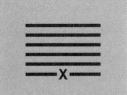

6 in the 1st place
Those who avoid evil, in both body
and mind, will have good fortune.

9 in the 2nd place
Those who deal with evil
themselves in order to protect
others will come to no harm.

9 in the 3rd place
There is danger, but no corruption
has occurred; no harm will be
done.

9 in the 4th place
Standing alone and impatient will
lead to evil.

9 in the 5th place
Patience and restraint until the
proper time will mean that
subsequent actions are effective.

9 at the top
Restricting one's action to non-
communication with evil will cause
regret, but no blame.

TS'UI

GATHERING TOGETHER

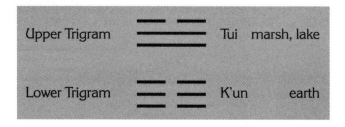

Upper Trigram		Tui marsh, lake
Lower Trigram		K'un earth

JUDGEMENT   Ts'ui represents collecting, or gathering together. Doing so in the correct way will bring success and gain in every action.

COMMENTARY   Ts'ui indicates the natural tendency of things to unite together.

SYMBOLISM   Ts'ui symbolises the necessity of keeping a union together.

LINES – TS'UI

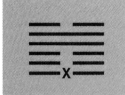

6 in the 1st place
When unable to achieve union oneself, seeking help will lead to success.

6 in the 2nd place
Being helped and encouraged by one who is stronger will bring good fortune.

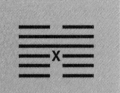

6 in the 3rd place
Despite difficulties, the wish for union will be successful, although some small regret will occur.

9 in the 4th place
Caution is needed for there to be success and no blame.

9 in the 5th place
Union has been achieved, but dignity will be needed in order to avoid any mistake.

6 at the top
If one is unable alone to achieve union, the desire for it will cause no error or blame.

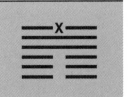

SHENG

ASCENDING

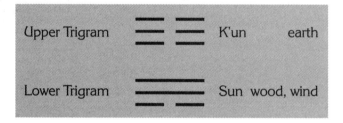

Upper Trigram	K'un	earth
Lower Trigram	Sun	wood, wind

JUDGEMENT　　Sheng represents moving upwards, or ascending. Modest determination will bring great progress and success.

COMMENTARY　　Sheng indicates gradual growth, leading to fulfilment.

SYMBOLISM　　Sheng symbolises the desirability of taking care of one's virtue and helping it to grow to maturity.

LINES – SHENG

6 in the 1st place
Modesty and a willingness to learn
will lead to improvement.

9 in the 2nd place
Sincerity and devoted loyalty do no
harm.

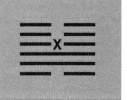

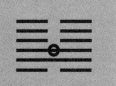

9 in the 3rd place
Bold and fearless progression is
presumptuous.

6 in the 4th place
Those who are deserving are
recognised; there will be good
fortune.

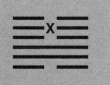

6 in the 5th place
Doing the right thing will lead to
easy advance and good fortune.

6 at the top
When everything has been
achieved, progressing further will
be fruitless.

K'UN

OPPRESSION

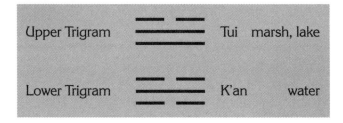

Upper Trigram		Tui	marsh, lake
Lower Trigram		K'an	water

JUDGEMENT

K'un represents oppression or the restraint of good by bad. Correctness is required for there to be success.

COMMENTARY

K'un indicates strength hidden by weakness. The person should do the right thing in order for the oppression to be lifted.

SYMBOLISM

K'un symbolises distress.

LINES – K'UN

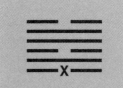

6 in the 1st place
Extreme stupidity will lead to
increased distress

9 in the 2nd place
During oppression, action will lead
to evil, although no blame will be
incurred.

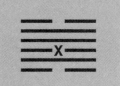

6 in the 3rd place
Reckless action will lead to
success.

9 in the 4th place
Any delay in giving help to others
will cause regret, but the outcome
will be good.

9 in the 5th place
Sincerity and flexibility will help to
overcome distress.

6 at the top
At the height of distress,
repentance will bring success.

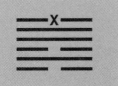

CHING

A WELL

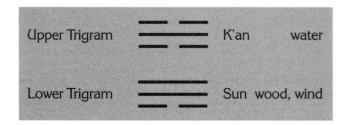

Upper Trigram		K'an	water
Lower Trigram		Sun	wood, wind

JUDGEMENT

Ching represents mutual helpfulness, as symbolised by the unchanging nature of a well, the value of which depends on the water being extracted from it.

COMMENTARY

Ching indicates that the bucket must reach the water and be drawn to the top safely for there to be any benefit.

SYMBOLISM

Ching symbolises the encouragement of others to help each other.

LINES – CHING

6 in the 1st place
Those who are corrupt and
incompetent will not be respected.

9 in the 2nd place
Lack of cooperation from others
will lead to failure.

9 in the 3rd place
Assistance that is available but not
taken will benefit no one.

6 in the 4th place
Self-absorbtion will benefit no one;
it will bring neither blame nor
praise.

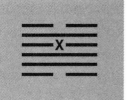

9 in the 5th place
Everyone draws upon what is
available; there will be fulfilment.

6 at the top
The general availability of benefits
will lead to great good fortune.

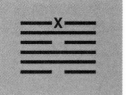

KO

—————————— REVOLUTION ——————————

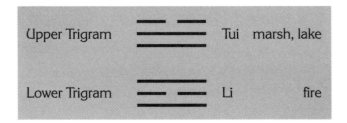

Upper Trigram		Tui	marsh, lake
Lower Trigram		Li	fire

JUDGEMENT   Ko represents the nature of necessary change. Change is viewed with suspicion and dislike until its effects are seen; only then is it believed in and accepted. Great progress and success will arise from the change, if both its motivation and result are good.

COMMENTARY   Ko indicates that people's dislike of change is overcome only in retrospect.

SYMBOLISM   Ko symbolises the need to choose properly the time for change.

LINES – KO

9 in the 1st place
Change made too early will make
any action impossible.

6 in the 2nd place
Action taken now to change things
will have fortunate results.

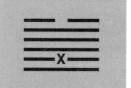

9 in the 3rd place
Reckless and violent change would
be dangerous. Caution and
thoughtfulness bring good results.

9 in the 4th place
If the confidence of others is
gained, action and change will be
advantageous.

9 in the 5th place
Change is believed in by others;
action will be advantageous.

6 at the top
The right thing to do is to avoid
solitary action; there will be good
fortune.

TING

THE CAULDRON

Upper Trigram	Li	fire
Lower Trigram	Sun	wood, wind

JUDGEMENT   Ting represents the nurturing of talents and virtue, leading to great progress and success.

COMMENTARY   Ting indicates how those who are deserving should be encouraged.

SYMBOLISM   Ting symbolises the need to follow the correct path in order that perfection be achieved.

LINES – TING

6 in the 1st place
Advantage will come from getting rid of what is bad; nothing will go wrong.

9 in the 2nd place
Caution will give enemies nothing to point at.

9 in the 3rd place
There is now failure, but doing the right thing will bring success in the end.

9 in the 4th place
Those who are not equal to the task and have no help will find it ends in failure.

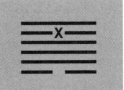

6 in the 5th place
Doing the right thing will bring gain.

9 at the top
Everything has been done; there will be great good fortune and any action will be beneficial.

CHEN

EXCITING POWER

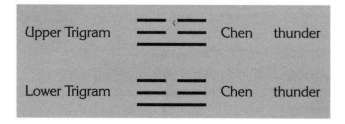

Upper Trigram		Chen	thunder
Lower Trigram		Chen	thunder

JUDGEMENT   Chen represents the way in which those most involved in times of change should behave. Only through care and precaution can danger be averted.

COMMENTARY   Chen indicates ease and development.

SYMBOLISM   Chen symbolises the necessity of cultivating one's virtues and examining one's faults.

LINES – CHEN

9 in the 1st place
When the correct time comes, apprehension will prove unfounded; there will be good fortune.

6 in the 2nd place
In times of danger, one should try to escape; things will eventually return to the way they were before.

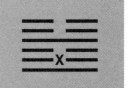

6 in the 3rd place
When one is distraught, action and movement will lead to no harm.

9 in the 4th place
There is nothing one can do; things will only get worse.

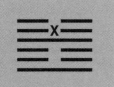

6 in the 5th place
Risk is always present, but safety will come in the end.

6 at the top
Action will lead to no good, but caution will reduce the consequences to blame.

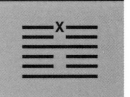

KEN

STOPPING MOVEMENT

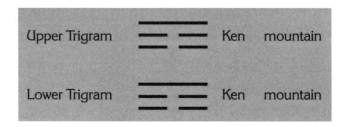

| Upper Trigram | Ken | mountain |
| Lower Trigram | Ken | mountain |

JUDGEMENT Ken represents resting or stopping; resting in what is right, or stopping by ceasing to move.

COMMENTARY Ken indicates resting when it is time to rest and acting when it is time to act. This will result in gain. There should be no self-consciousness in resting or moving.

SYMBOLISM Ken symbolises the need to confine one's actions to those suitable in one's position in life.

LINES – KEN

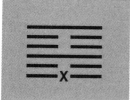

6 in the 1st place
From the beginning, only what is right should be done; no harm will come of this and caution will lead to gain.

6 in the 2nd place
Dissatisfaction will come from being unable to help others.

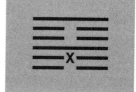

9 in the 3rd place
There is danger; disorder and anger will occur.

6 in the 4th place
The self alone can be kept from agitation; nothing will go wrong.

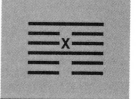

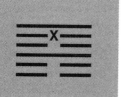

6 in the 5th place
Those who are not hasty in what they say will have no need to repent.

9 at the top
Restfulness, generosity and goodness will lead to good fortune.

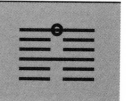

CHIE/N
GRADUAL PROGRESS

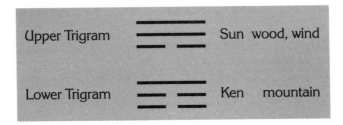

Upper Trigram		Sun wood, wind
Lower Trigram		Ken mountain

JUDGEMENT   Chien represents gradual progress or growth. Doing the right thing will lead to gain.

COMMENTARY   Chien indicates gradual progress where each step is properly carried out from beginning to end.

SYMBOLISM   Chien symbolises how extraordinary goodness may be achieved and maintained by the gradual nature of its growth.

LINES – CHIEN

6 in the 1st place
Danger exists through circumstances, not one's own actions; nothing will go wrong.

6 in the 2nd place
Rest and fulfilment, if earned, will lead to good fortune.

9 in the 3rd place
Strength, though failing in duty, will be useful in the end.

6 in the 4th place
Modesty and right will overcome any shortcomings; nothing will go wrong.

9 in the 5th place
Though a victim of circumstances, one will experience good fortune in the end.

9 at the top
After everything is done, other usefulness will lead to good fortune.

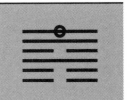

KUEI MEI

DECENCY

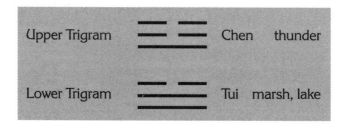

Upper Trigram		Chen	thunder
Lower Trigram		Tui	marsh, lake

JUDGEMENT   Kuei Mei represents decency and the way that lapses in decency will lead to harm.

COMMENTARY   Kuei Mei indicates that care should be taken to ensure that decency is maintained from the beginning, so that nothing bad will occur in the end.

SYMBOLISM   Kuei Mei symbolises the way that small lapses in decency may lead to greater harm.

LINES – KUEI MEI

9 in the 1st place
Despite apparent shortcomings, good service will lead to good fortune.

9 in the 2nd place
Faithful devotion will make up for other shortcomings; there will be benefits.

6 in the 3rd place
Meanness and indecency will lead to loss of position.

9 in the 4th place
Proper delay will lead to a better result.

6 in the 5th place
Placing oneself second to another will lead to good fortune.

6 at the top
When the decent thing is not done, there will be failure and no benefits.

FENG

PROSPERITY

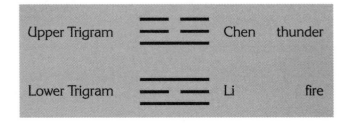

Upper Trigram		Chen	thunder
Lower Trigram		Li	fire

JUDGEMENT   Feng represents abundance and prosperity, which in turn bring lack of anxiety and therefore progress and development.

COMMENTARY   Feng indicates the nature of prosperity. It is the nature of all things to change, and therefore prosperity will change to poverty.

SYMBOLISM   Feng symbolises the necessity of being correct and exact in all judgements.

LINES – FENG

9 in the 1st place
Prosperity will be maintained by
helping one another.

6 in the 2nd place
Advice to others will be treated
with suspicion; sincerity is needed
for there to be success.

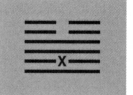

9 in the 3rd place
Great things should not be
attempted, but in trying to do the
right thing, mistakes will be
avoided.

9 in the 4th place
Even in darkness, meeting of like
with like will lead to good fortune.

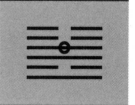

6 in the 5th place
If one is helped by others, the
result will be admirable and there
will be good fortune.

6 at the top
Those who are selfish and solitary
will be ostracised; no one will help
and the result will be bad.

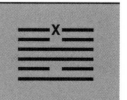

LU

TRAVELLING STRANGER

Upper Trigram	Li	fire
Lower Trigram	Ken	mountain

JUDGEMENT

Lu represents travelling and how those who travel should behave. Those who are modest and honest will avoid harm and achieve progress.

COMMENTARY

Lu indicates the qualities needed in a traveller: restfulness, modesty and intelligence.

SYMBOLISM

Lu symbolises the use of wisdom and caution in all judgements.

LINES – LU

6 in the 1st place
Selfishness and meanness will
bring about disaster.

6 in the 2nd place
When equipped with everything
that is needed, there will be no
cause for complaint.

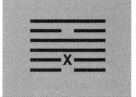

9 in the 3rd place
Arrogance and violence towards
others will put the person in
danger.

9 in the 4th place
Despite being protected against
danger, one's own caution will give
rise to apprehension.

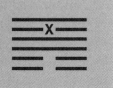

6 in the 5th place
Good qualities will bring praise
from others.

9 at the top
Arrogant behaviour and deafness
to what is right will lead to harm.

SUN

──────── *GENTLE PENETRATION* ────────

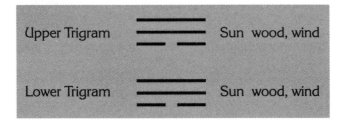

| Upper Trigram | | Sun wood, wind |
| Lower Trigram | | Sun wood, wind |

JUDGEMENT Sun represents the process of gently correcting and improving. From this will come achievement and progress in small degrees, leading to advantage in any direction.

COMMENTARY Sun indicates the relationship between those in authority and those who are willing to accept orders when they are given to make changes for the better.

SYMBOLISM Sun symbolises the agreement of people to follow orders that are right and just.

LINES – SUN

6 in the 1st place
Those who are confused feel the
need for a lead from others.

9 in the 2nd place
A genuine aim will overcome any
distractions and lead to good
fortune.

9 in the 3rd place
Restlessness and violence will be
ineffective, and will lead to regret.

6 in the 4th place
Everything has been achieved,
leading to success.

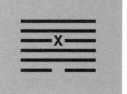

9 in the 5th place
Flexibility and the wish to do what
is right will bring good fortune.

9 at the top
Any attempt to do the right thing
that is not based on fairness will
result in harm.

TUI

—— *JOY, PLEASURE* ——

Upper Trigram		Tui	marsh, lake
Lower Trigram		Tui	marsh, lake

JUDGEMENT   Tui represents pleasure or satisfaction. It is essential to do the right thing in order for there to be progress and attainment.

COMMENTARY   Tui indicates satisfaction. People are willing to endure hard work and face danger to reach this position.

SYMBOLISM   Tui symbolises the value of encouraging friendship and union.

LINES – TUI

9 in the 1st place
Nothing has yet been done which can be judged; inner harmony will lead to good fortune.

9 in the 2nd place
There will not be any incorrect action; sincerity will bring good fortune.

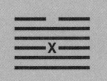

6 in the 3rd place
Excessive and selfish pursuit of pleasure will lead to evil.

9 in the 4th place
Reflection and deliberation, before giving in to pleasure, will bring joy.

9 in the 5th place
Those who trust someone who would injure them will face danger.

6 at the top
There is pleasure in attracting and leading others; but intentions must remain good throughout.

HUAN

DISPERSION

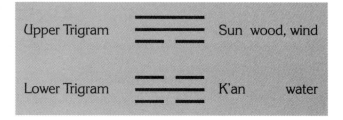

Upper Trigram   Sun   wood, wind

Lower Trigram   K'an   water

JUDGEMENT   Huan represents dispersion or dissipation. This takes the form of moving away from what is right and good. Sincere faith is needed to remedy this fault. Dangerous tasks can then be undertaken, provided that right is present.

COMMENTARY   Huan indicates the progress and success that will be attained by remaining true to what is right.

SYMBOLISM   Huan symbolises the necessity of faith in fighting this tendency to move away from what is right.

LINES – HUAN

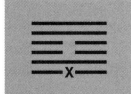

6 in the 1st place
Weakness will need help to deal
with the beginnings of what is bad.
There will be good fortune.

9 in the 2nd place
Seeking union will give shelter
from harm.

6 in the 3rd place
Those who are fearlessly selfless
will have no need to repent.

6 in the 4th place
Dispersion or scattering, followed
by the collection of the best
elements, will bring great good
fortune.

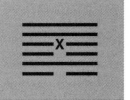

9 in the 5th place
As perspiration flows from the
body, so will correct orders flow
from goodness.

9 at the top
Those who avoid danger will not
be blamed.

CHIEH

CONTROL

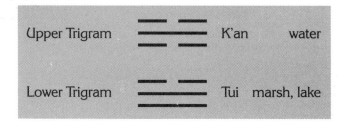

| Upper Trigram | | K'an | water |
| Lower Trigram | | Tui | marsh, lake |

JUDGEMENT
Chieh represents control, or restraint. If this control fits in with circumstances and is not too severe, it will lead to permanent success and attainment.

COMMENTARY
Chieh indicates the temporary nature of rules that are too severe, in that they cannot be maintained.

SYMBOLISM
Chieh symbolises that excessive restraint will cause those who are restrained to lose their tolerance.

LINES – CHIEH

9 in the 1st place
Those who are not hasty and
remain calm will do no wrong.

9 in the 2nd place
Remaining inactive when it is time
to act will lead to evil.

6 in the 3rd place
The realisation that failure to obey
rules leads to blame will come too
late. There will be sorrow.

6 in the 4th place
Quiet acceptance of authority will
lead to progress and success.

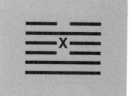

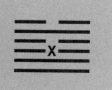

9 in the 5th place
Those who follow the rules
willingly will have good fortune.

6 at the top
Those in authority who are too
severe will finally repent; the
situation will improve.

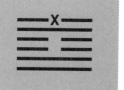

CHUNG FU
───────────── *INNER SINCERITY* ─────────────

Upper Trigram		Sun wood, wind
Lower Trigram		Tui marsh, lake

JUDGEMENT   Chung Fu represents the high quality of inner sincerity. Lack of preoccupation and selfishness will lead to gain.

COMMENTARY   Chung Fu indicates the power of sincerity to bring about a happy state of cooperation between people.

SYMBOLISM   Chung Fu symbolises the ability of sincerity to address even the deepest questions or problems.

LINES – CHUNG FU

9 in the 1st place
Friendly sincerity within the self will
bring good fortune.

9 in the 2nd place
A deep love of sincerity will unite
people in a common cause.

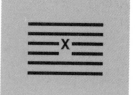

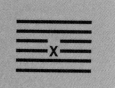

6 in the 3rd place
Sincerity not kept to the self will be
open to outside influence; there
will be confusion.

6 in the 4th place
Discarding distracting influences
will lead to greater sincerity.

9 in the 5th place
Sincerity, bringing about close
union with others, will do no harm.

9 at the top
Ineffectual movements, no matter
how correct, will lead to harm.

HSAIO KUO
SMALL EXCESSES

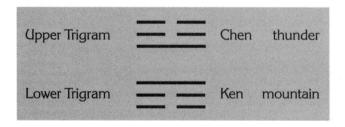

| Upper Trigram | Chen | thunder |
| Lower Trigram | Ken | mountain |

JUDGEMENT Hsaio Kuo represents the fact that small excesses in matters which are not essential to correctness are allowed.

COMMENTARY Hsaio Kuo indicates that small excesses may be carried out in small affairs and there will be good fortune.

SYMBOLISM Hsaio Kuo symbolises the correctness of great humility and economy.

LINES – HSAIO KUO

6 in the 1st place
An excessive lack of humility will
unavoidably lead to harm.

6 in the 2nd place
Those who proceed in a modest
and loyal way will do no wrong.

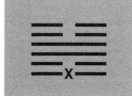

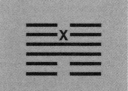

9 in the 3rd place
Overconfidence and a lack of
defensive measures will lead
to harm.

9 in the 4th place
Proceeding will be dangerous; it is
best to avoid excessive action.

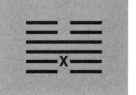

6 in the 5th place
There is danger, but no harm will
come of it.

6 at the top
Those who overstep the line are
asking for trouble.

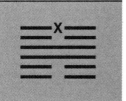

CHI CHI
COMPLETION

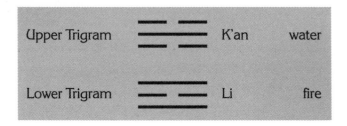

| Upper Trigram | | K'an | water |
| Lower Trigram | | Li | fire |

JUDGEMENT   Chi Chi represents completion, or successful accomplishment. The correct course must be followed as things are now naturally unstable; order is usually followed by disorder.

COMMENTARY   Chi Chi indicates the nature of change; order changes to disorder and disorder to order.

SYMBOLISM   Chi Chi symbolises the need to anticipate what is bad and take precautions against it.

LINES – CHI CHI

9 in the 1st place
After accomplishment should
come rest; nothing will go wrong.

6 in the 2nd place
Action would now be wrong; what
is lost will eventually be found, at
the appropriate time.

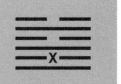

9 in the 3rd place
Long and tedious actions, despite
their successful outcome, will lead
to weariness.

6 in the 4th place
Caution is needed; precautions
against what is bad would be wise.

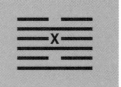

9 in the 5th place
Patience and caution, with
sincerity, will bring great good
fortune.

6 at the top
Violent action at this time will lead
to danger.

WEI CHI
——————BEFORE COMPLETION——————

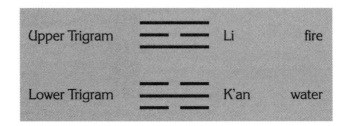

Upper Trigram		Li	fire
Lower Trigram		K'an	water

JUDGEMENT   Wei Chi represents a time prior to completion, before what is desired has been achieved. In terms of the nature of change, it represents a time when order has turned to disorder and the struggle to achieve order has begun again.

COMMENTARY   Wei Chi indicates that lack of caution in attempting to deal with disorder will lead to failure. With caution will come progress and success.

SYMBOLISM   Wei Chi symbolises lack of harmony and order.

LINES – WEI CHI

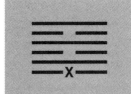

6 in the 1st place
Ignorant attempts at action will
give cause for regret.

9 in the 2nd place
Those who do the right thing and
practise restraint will have good
fortune.

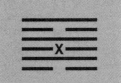

6 in the 3rd place
Proceeding before the situation is
remedied will lead to harm.

9 in the 4th place
Correct and vigorous efforts to
deal with disorder will be
encouraged and will lead to good
fortune.

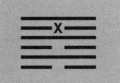

6 in the 5th place
Sincerity and modesty will lead to
good fortune.

9 at the top
Confidence and quiet enjoyment
of success will cause no harm;
overaction will lead to misfortune.

Index